Finding Purpose in 15 Minutes

By

Derrick Drakeford, MPA

Published by
Drakeford, Scott, & Associates L.L.C.
Durham, North Carolina

Acknowledgements

This book is intended for all people and it is written carefully not to offend your belief system or infer mine on yours. It is written out of a passion to help individuals, families, and organizations chart a purposeful path. I write to my friends who do not believe in God, my neighbors of different beliefs, and my friends who are Islamic. I thank my mentors here on earth and those who have gone on, who opened my eyes to myself and to the world in new and challenging ways. I thank God for inspiration and my wife Iris for her patience and love. My father Dr. Robert Wayne Drakeford, my pastor Rev. Dr. Quincy Scott Jr., Dr. James Brooks, and Anthony Austin.

To my mother Diane, my brother Bobby and most of all my God sent wife Iris and her patience with me in this work.
To my friends Reco, Andrea, Angela, Marcus, Dan, Mark, and the countless others who have poured into my life.

Contents

Introduction

There I sat with my head in my hands calmly resting my temples on my thumbprints. For some reason sitting in the unemployment office for the second time in as many years was not that bad anymore. I wasn't filled with depression and despair as I was before. My mind was not clouded with doubt, fear, and a sense of loss of control as before. My circumstances mirrored one of my life's most painful experiences, and yet this time I felt no pain. It was quite the contrary, my soul was bubbling with hope and limitless opportunity. I thought to myself "*I Have Limitless Opportunity*", while a competing thought said 'you are a Black man on the unemployment line how can you see this jaded world as *Limitless Opportunity.*

For some reason this time I did. Something had changed inside of me in those past two years. My search for self had landed on solid ground. The quest for meaning was etching out a beautiful tapestry. My steps were ordered and I felt that even these steps through the unemployment line _again_ were drenched in meaning and purpose. This transformation over the past two years had given me eye surgery. I now saw the same things but did not interpret them in the same light. This new passion and a confidence, in my uniquely God given gifts, became the unspoken answer to the multitude of questions that circled my mind.

In taking those two years to deeply self examine my painful experiences, and process through my contributions to my environment I found my Purpose in Life. I now embraced pain and circumstances with a newly healed heart and a positive outlook on my abilities. It still hurt, I could still feel the pain, but I didn't feel as lonely and as hopeless as I did before. My colleague at Shaw University Dr. William Thurston would always say, "_Our purpose is birthed from our pain._"

> _Our purpose is birthed from our pain_

I understood what he said because I was finally able to honestly analyze my painful experiences.

Reverend Dr. Martin Luther King, Jr. said *'our lives are all tied together in a single garment of destiny'*. More than ever I felt like a valued part of that garment and was charged to play my role in healing and rebuilding the cracks and snares left on humanity.

Through this process I developed a simple activity that helps all people by looking at life through the conceptual framework of a box (or set of proven principal parameters). I found this was more effective than the trend of living outside the box… which is code for…making it up as you go along. I had realized that I needed a sense of purpose to insulate my emotional trauma in order to create shelter from the winds of poor circumstances. I needed fundamental beliefs in my self and my surroundings that centrally motivated and guided my life's work. I concluded that I had a role to play in my own destiny and I loved it. I found there was no way this feeling could coexist with my former thoughts of victimization, racial inferiority-then superiority, and a general feeling of being lost on earth.

I gleaned that the process I was going through internally had mirrored the searches of other great people whose lives were filled with meaning and sacrifice. I thought if I could encapsulate these lessons I learned in finding my own purpose in life, I could effectively teach others in their self-navigation process to purpose. This activity would add value to other's lives. Through trial and error, contextual research, and personal observations of my teaching results with over 1,000 undergraduate students, graduate students, and adult learners I was able to whittle down a **self examination activity that takes only fifteen minutes to help people of all ages find their purpose in life.**

The following chapters chronicle the lessons found in my own search for purpose and my career as a college professor, organizational consultant, business coach, and nonprofit trainer. The activity in this book can be used for self examination, team building, and community development. I hope you enjoy your journey as much as I still do. Feel free to drop me an email and let me know how you are using this new resource. (ddrakeford@drakefordassociates.org)

-With Love Derrick Rudolph Drakeford

Three Points of View

This book contains three different ways for participants to process the activity. These three points of view are just three different ways a participant can look at the activity, pick which one fits best and operate from a point of view that is the most natural for you.

Faith Point of View

When I teach about Purpose I have found most people will inevitably end up talking about God. For many of us our internal definition of purpose is filtered through our learned and experienced faith beliefs. There is a group that sees God as the 'strict puppet master' pulling the strings of life connected to our circumstances. This group may also interpret individual purpose as pointless to determine because people don't have an essential role in the outcome.

I however, see God as all loving, forgiving, the essence of empathy and support, and therefore much of my understanding of *Purpose* is filtered through my lenses of faith. My goal in writing this book is not to proselytize on what is the right or wrong view of faith. The intent is to spur the internal probing questions that when seriously contemplated give us all a framework in which to interpret Purpose for ourselves in our environments. It has value when applied in the context of real life and our impact on community. Our discussion in the activity only works when it is followed by acts that serve the community.

For people who are navigating fulfilled lives with a healthy, productive, and nonviolent expression of faith, I suggest you interpret the concepts in this activity through the paradigm of your faith. Many people are in the natural process grappling with questions and concepts of faith. We all see ultra religious people making moral mistakes and even the worst kinds of weapons for mass death in the name of their god. I understand where these critiques are coming from. Instead of throwing this activity out with the religious self-help material, it may be more effective if you interpret the activity through a nonreligious point of view, such as utility or value added.

Utility Point of View

Utility basically means 'use' or usefulness. In the end that's what purpose boils down to ..."Usefulness".

We look at the world through these eyes. *What is it good for? How can it be used to help people?*

I suggest we look at our examination of Purpose in Life, by asking ourselves the question: What makes me uniquely useful and how can I perfect that talent? What is my internal gold (precious item) that opens doors for me and makes me uniquely important? This activity will help to answer the following questions:

1. Why do some people recognize my talent and others don't?

2. How can I position myself to be where my talent is best used?

Value Added Point of View (Entrepreneurship)

Another healthy way to look at this activity is through the Value Added Point of View. This looks at what value a product or service adds to others lives, or in the case of businesses to the marketplace. For example the genius of science and the brilliance of math brings together creations like "smart phones" which are made for the specific purpose of adding new services to the average phone, which now make the device more valuable to the user.

> *The person who knows how to build the machine brings an added value.*

A mentor of my mine Dr. Kelly Hill says "even the person who make fries at McDonalds adds value to those of us who consume the fries, but the person who knows how to build or fix the machine that fries the fries brings an added value. There are a finite number of people who can fix the machine versus frying the fries".

This point of view makes *value added* the blossoms of the flower called purpose. Once individuals are steeped in purpose they move toward their destiny with vigor and passion. It is it harder for these purpose-identified people to get in trouble through senseless activity like, violence, abuse, or negligence. It is only when we loose our confidence in our purpose and our innate abilities that we feel our lives and our talents add no value. This negative thinking causes us to make poor decisions.

Through the Value Added point of view, our value can be quantified and strategically developed to make ourselves (and the product or service we provide) even more valuable. This is one of the main reasons to pursue college, trade school, and apprenticeship study. It is the ability to become even more proficient at our talent. This process allows our talent to become more valuable to people and to the marketplace. When I was teaching at The Shaw University in Raleigh North Carolina, I would have an overwhelming amount of the same inquires from students in my classes. They would ask me "Mr. Drakeford how can learning this make me money or get a job". This common question was rooted in the essential inquiry on purpose and how making money to support one's family is foundational to surviving, providing, and thriving in the American market economy. The question is a good one, because it forces us to answer how does the development of my skills help me to make money, and effectively navigate the marketplace. This question becomes more perplexing in the midst of seeing rap stars and reality TV actors making a lot of money with little to no skill development.

Value and money are positively correlated so even untalented reality TV stars add value to their faithful viewers (even if it makes the viewers themselves feel better about their own talents). Each of us has a role to play in adding value to others lives, our communities, and the world. The role we play can be measured through the performance of a job, the sales of a product or service, or word of mouth recommendations for the quality of our work. The key is not to allow the circumstances, pressures, and cravings of money to sidetrack our forward progress towards adding value to others. The Value Added Point of

View is a viable way for each of us to look at this activity in our search towards answering the questions:

"What value do I add to my community?"

"What in the world am I here for?"

Activity: *Finding Your Purpose in 15 Minutes*

To find your purpose in fifteen minutes it requires an honest and transparent self-examination of gifts, painful experiences and the environment. The following three questions help us to frame purpose in a way that's easy to understand and implement in everyday life. These questions force us to come to a definitive answer quicker than philosophical rhetoric.

We start the activity by drawing a four-quadrant box on a sheet of paper (as depicted below in Figure 1) that will serve as a conceptual framework to map out our purpose.

Figure 1

Question 1: Quadrant I

People- who are the people closest to your heart?

What is the community of choice that you most closely identify with and your heart feels compassion for. When you see this group in pain you feel their pain, as if it were yours and your heart spurs to help this group of people. The pain this group feels may keep you up some nights. Examples of communities of choice are:

1. Handicapped people
2. Elderly people
3. At-risk youth
4. Children
5. Homeless people
6. Orphans from third world countries
7. Animals/ pets
8. The environment, etc.

For this activity we generally define this group as the People we are purposed to help.

List this group or groups in bullet format in Quadrant I as depicted below. As you can see I have listed my People, or community of choice below. My first 'community of choice' is *Lost People*, which I define as individuals of all ages who have not yet identified their purpose in life, which prevents them from sustained fulfillment (for me, many times this represents young black men). The second group I have identified is Lost Organizations, which I define as organization's experiencing mission drift or questioning their long-term strategic plan and usefulness to the community or marketplace.

Figure 2

People • Lost People • Lost Organizations	

Question 2: Quadrant III

What is the pain that you have experience in your life that changed the way that you looked at the world forever?

By examining your own life experiences determine the pain that you most identify with. What is the experience that was so powerful that you decided from this moment on you will dedicate your life to alleviating or preventing that pain from occurring in other people lives, especially the people you just identified in question #1. The pain this specific group experiences is something that you identify with because it is similar to some painful experience that happened so close to you that you could feel it. This pain may have tried to define you mentally and cause you to wrestle with the most essential questions of life, fairness, and purpose. Such as the questions;

From this moment on you will dedicate your life to alleviating or preventing that pain

* What on earth am I here for?
* What is my purpose?

- Why does my heart beat?

- Why do I wake up with breath in the morning and others don't.

For me that pain was being a *Lost Person* and feeling that I didn't have definitive future. As I think on my childhood I realize that my parent's divorce was a defining painful experience that shaped the internal questions, I would wrestle with for years. These questions came full circle when I found myself highly qualified and unable to obtain gainful employment. I felt lost <u>again</u>, I was worried, alone and longing for mentorship in new ways that would enable me to use my gifts to find a path to success in the marketplace.

> *I felt lost again, I was worried, alone and longing for mentorship*

It was during my time on the faculty at Shaw University that I realized most if not all of my students were also carrying scars from childhood pain that directly related to their ability to succeed and impact their community of choice.

In the following chart (Figure 3) I list my painful experiences in quadrant III

Figure 3

People
  • Lost People
  • Lost Organizations	

Pain
  • Lost feeling from parents divorce
  • Lost feeling from unemployment
  • Lost feeling from failed relationships	

Pain's Healing Process- Making Peace

Depression is the result of pain that remains in the mind and emotions too long. It is essential to our purpose in life to process through our pain in order to come out on the other side healthy, functioning, and useful. If we do not properly navigate the healing process we will become bitter, cynical, and generally not fun to be around. This process gives individuals the ability and confidence to help others in their own healing. This is where the pain starts to come full circle and becomes vital to the cyclical process of helping others. When we give, the giver

> *If we do not properly navigate the healing process we will become bitter*

receives so much more than the recipient. The mere act of giving positions the giver in a posture of a nurturer and allows the giver and the recipient to lower their emotional walls to become truly vulnerable. This ability to be vulnerable, open, and communicative is essential to building effective teams and relationships.

My friend Marcus Tyrance recently attended the Congressional Black Caucus Foundation's national conference. At one of the brain trust sessions he heard George Frazier say 'employees shouldn't feel bad if they are feeling used. We should feel bad if we are not being used because that means we have lost our usefulness".

I believe <u>Usefulness</u> if the Fullness of Utility, the peek of ability. This is where talent and opportunity collide to create destiny. Through analyzing and moving past our pain we become more useful to others.

Peace Process

The process to heal and transition out of paralyzing emotional pain is the transformation from pain to peace. Living at peace means operating in a state of mind where we are aware of our painful experiences, but no longer allow them to define us. For each of us this process is different. For me, faith assists my healing process through prayer, and forgiveness. In most cases it is myself that I must forgive first before I can move on and become productive again. When I pray it helps me to realize God's immense size, omnipotence, and ability to carry my pain on his shoulders. This grace, to embrace me with love after all the things I've done that I'm not proud of, and the many times I misrepresented god, my family, and my self.

> *Remove this pain from your mental and emotional plate*

Others go through this process by meditation, conversation, writing rhymes, relaxation, or exercise. Professional counseling can offer the opportunity to talk out the pain to a qualified professional, who can suggest healthy coping strategies. The key is to begin the process to remove this pain from your mental and emotional plate. An empty plate is the prerequisite needed to replace this pain with a purposeful experience that fills our hearts with the promise and beauty of life.

When doing this exercise with a class I draw an arrow from Quadrant III to Quadrant II and write the word "Peace" (See Figure 4) on the line to symbolize the internal process of emotionally dumping my pain in order to become productive and impactful towards the community closest to my heart.

Figure 4

People • Lost People • Lost Organizations	
PEACE PROCESS	
Pain • Lost feeling from parents divorce • Lost feeling from unemployment • Lost feeling from failed relationships	

Question 3: Quadrant II

Passion

Now that we have examined our *People* our *Pain* and begun our healing process, we explore *Passion*. This is your unique talent, or gift set that allows you to effectively serve your community of choice. It intrigues me how the world has billions of people all with a unique thumbprint. As unique as your thumbprint, your gifts reflect a similar imprint on the world. Your passion represents, things that come easy to you but hard to other people. It is something you enjoy doing that can also be used to help the *People* (Community of Choice) alleviate or prevent the *Pain* (They go through and you identify with). When I do this exercise with teens, or adults passion is always the easiest to examine. For some reason every participant in my classes

> *Things that come easy to you but hard to other people*

have at some point in time taken serious thought to the questions "What am I passionate about?" or "What is my Talent?" When we think about it this time try not to regurgitate your prior self-examinations on passion, but instead place it in relations to your answers for *People* and *Pain*.

My passion is communication (See Figure 5). I use written and oral communication to help lost people (like myself), prevent the pain associated with feeling lost.

I practically do this through my for-profit company Drakeford, Scott, & Associates L.L.C., which provides;

strategic planning, motivational speaking, board development, and grant writing. I also do this alongside other experts through a nonprofit corporation CommunityMindedConsulting.org. This is a nonprofit designed to walk individuals through the process of starting a business or nonprofit which drastically improves their community.

It took me a while but I finally found a purposeful path to use my gifts to help the *People* I was created to help.

Figure 5

People
• Lost People
• Lost Organizations
	Passion
	• Communication
	  ▪ Writing
	  ▪ Training
	  ▪ Strategic Planning

Pain • Lost feeling from parents divorce • Lost feeling from unemployment • Lost feeling from failed relationships	= PURPOSE

Use this equation to find your purpose in fifteen minutes

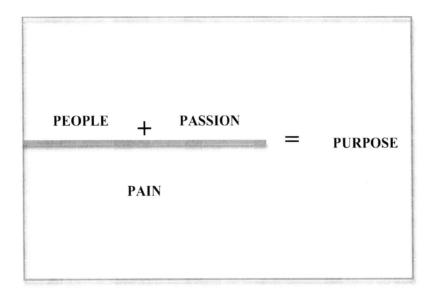

*The line represents the continual Peace Process

Conclusion

As promised this activity was quick and relatively painless, but it offers us a framework in which to constantly review our purpose in life. As my father says "you may have multiple purposes in your lifetime as it progresses," so don't get stuck on your initial analysis revisit these internal probing questions to make sure you are on the right path.

This activity also works for team building and mission development. I have found that when others know your purpose they know how to work best with you. Cornel West says and I concur, "that at the end of our life the only meaningful accomplishments we will have is the quality of our relationships and the work we have accomplished together".